EASY SPANISH VOCABULARY PUZZLES

EASY SPANISH VOCABULARY PUZZLES

Jane Burnett Smith

Printed on recyclable paper

PASSPORT BOOKS
a division of *NTC Publishing Group*
Lincolnwood, Illinois USA

1995 Printing

Published by Passport Books, a division of NTC Publishing Group.
©1991 by NTC Publishing Group, 4255 West Touhy Avenue,
Lincolnwood (Chicago), Illinois 60646-1975 U.S.A.
Manufactured in the United States of America.

5 6 7 8 9 VP 9 8 7 6 5

Preface

Easy Spanish Vocabulary Puzzles is an entertaining collection of word games and puzzles for students of Spanish and anyone who wants to brush up. These puzzles will amuse you as well as help you increase your Spanish vocabulary.

The puzzles were created with the advanced beginning or intermediate learner in mind. Divided into six sections, they cover common topics, such as food, plants and animals, and daily life. These topics are generally taught in basic Spanish courses and will be useful to anyone who wishes to communicate in Spanish.

The puzzles also come in a variety of fun formats to keep your interest high. In this book, you will find crossword puzzles, bilingual anagrams, word searches, and much more to challenge you. You will find that as you work through the book, the puzzles become increasingly difficult. Learners at different levels will find a variety of puzzles within their abilities. Or you can simply start with the easiest puzzles and work your way to the most challenging ones. However you choose to proceed, each puzzle is accompanied by clear instructions in English and Spanish, so that you can do them in the order that suits you best.

Do these puzzles by yourself or share them with friends. Either way, *Easy Spanish Vocabulary Puzzles* will bring you hours of enjoyment as well as improving your Spanish vocabulary. And remember, when you are finished with a puzzle, you can check your solutions in the Answer Key at the back of the book.

Contents

Section 4 ✍ ★ ✍ Sección 4
Language • El lenguaje

Section 5 ✍ ★ ✍ Sección 5
Daily Life • La vida cotidiana

Section 6 ✍ ★ ✍ Sección 6
Recreation and Sports • El recreo y los deportes

Index of Puzzles by Type

Bilingual Anagrams *Anagramas bilingües*

Bilingual Crossword *Crucigrama bilingüe*

Drop and Add *Quite y añada*

Labyrinth *Laberinto*

Word Cross ✍ Palabras cruzadas

Word Search ✍ Buscapalabras

Section 1

Sección 1

Flora and Fauna

★

Flora y fauna

Plants and Animals ★ Plantas y animales

Swallow		Pheasant	
Pansy		Poplar	
Crow		Willow	**SAUCE**
Daisy		Horse	
Elephant		Carnation	

Translate the English words into Spanish. Write the Spanish words in the horizontal spaces. They all pertain to the classification represented by the vertical phrase.

Traduzca las palabras inglesas al español. Escriba las palabras españolas en los espacios horizontales. Todas pertenecen a la clasificación representada por la frase vertical.

Birds and Animals ★ Aves y animales

```
A  V  E  S  T  R  U  Z  J  Ó  Y  O
L  G  B  A  P  O  A  J  E  V  O  R
O  W  O  L  A  B  L  F  G  T  S  R
T  P  Á  L  L  M  A  L  A  K  N  E
R  A  G  I  O  Y  A  G  A  P  A  P
Ó  R  U  D  M  N  A  O  E  B  G  B
T  D  I  R  A  L  D  R  U  L  A  E
Q  N  L  A  L  R  I  R  O  H  Y  C
E  O  A  I  E  C  S  B  I  T  X  E
G  L  N  C  O  E  O  R  F  N  H  R
T  A  C  U  G  A  V  I  O  T  A  R
A  B  O  L  I  R  D  O  C  O  C  O
```

Translate the words into Spanish. Look in the puzzle for the words you have written in the list. They may be situated horizontally, vertically, or diagonally, forward or backward. Draw a circle around each word you find and write an X beside the word in the list.

Traduzca las palabras al español. Busque en la sopa de letras todas las palabras que haya escrito en la lista. Pueden situarse horizontal, vertical o diagonalmente, en un sentido o el opuesto. Dibuje un círculo alrededor de cada palabra que encuentre y escriba una X al lado de la palabra de la lista.

Horse	_____	Sea gull	_____
Pig	_____	Ostrich	_____
Squirrel	_____	Swallow	_____
Wolf	LOBO	Turtledove	_____
Crocodile	_____	Cat	_____
Calf	_____	Parrot	_____
Sheep	_____	Eagle	_____
Hen	_____	Goose	_____
Dove	_____	Dog	_____
Lark	_____	Parakeet	_____

3

More Birds and Animals ★ Más aves y animales

The clues are written in Spanish. Write the answers in English in the puzzle.

Los indicios están escritos en español. Escriba las soluciones en inglés en el crucigrama.

Horizontal

1. Águila
5. Cerdo
8. Aceite
9. Egotismo; el yo
10. Burro
12. Ciudad de California (*abrev.*)
13. Oveja
14. Animal de la casa
15. Ella
17. Perro
19. Ayudado
23. ¡Está bien! (*abrev.*)
24. Una gata persa
25. Olmo
27. El; la
28. Decir
29. Pavonear

Vertical

1. Termina
2. Ido
3. Gusta
4. Animales gigantes
5. Ese hombre
6. Ojear
7. Cabra
11. Exclamación
16. Ocho
17. Hace
18. Estado al norte de Texas (*abrev.*)
20. El que hace
21. Terminación comparativa
22. Saeta
26. Mi

Scrambled Flora and Fauna ★ Flora y fauna revueltas

In the first column are the scrambled letters of words in English and Spanish. In the second column are the English words. Cross out the letters of each English word in the first column. With the remaining letters, form the equivalent word in Spanish. Write the word in the third column. Follow the model.

En la primera columna hay las letras revueltas de palabras en inglés y español. En la segunda columna hay las palabras en inglés. Tache las letras de cada palabra inglesa en la primera columna. De las letras restantes, forme la palabra equivalente en español. Pase la palabra a la tercera columna. Siga el modelo.

MODEL: ~~HONAMNAD~~ HAND _____MANO_____

1.	APLYOAPOAPMP	POPPY	_____
2.	UBSOPAURELLCOD	ROSEBUD	_____
3.	BABJEINTORCO	RABBIT	_____
4.	FRAZOXOR	FOX	_____
5.	RASOBEO	BEAR	_____
6.	EJAPEOVESH	SHEEP	_____
7.	WACCOVA	COW	_____
8.	ELACYEABBARD	BARLEY	_____
9.	ZOMARÍNC	CORN	_____
10.	MADVAOPELO	DOVE	_____
11.	GONTALOCODÓNT	COTTON	_____
12.	ILÁGULEAGEA	EAGLE	_____
13.	GIAFIUGHER	FIG (TREE)	_____
14.	SEACHOORBALL	HORSE	_____
15.	GLOWLANTAUN	WALNUT (TREE)	_____
16.	BALGOCCEBA	CABBAGE	_____
17.	VAPTOKERUY	TURKEY	_____
18.	TIARSADGARIAMY	DAISY	_____
19.	LORPOTRARO	PARROT	_____
20.	ISPSNORBTAUN	TURNIPS	_____

Nature ★ La naturaleza

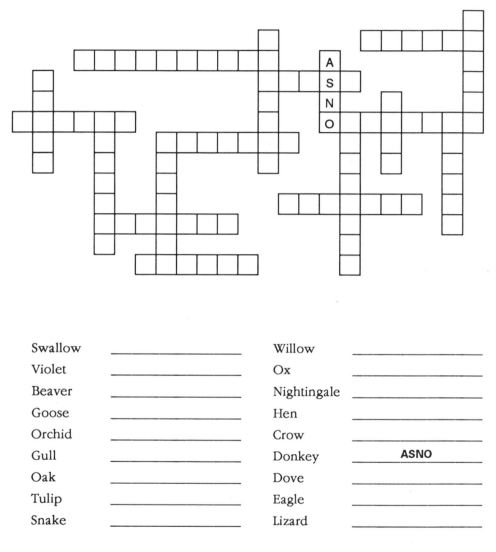

Swallow	_____	Willow	_____
Violet	_____	Ox	_____
Beaver	_____	Nightingale	_____
Goose	_____	Hen	_____
Orchid	_____	Crow	_____
Gull	_____	Donkey	**ASNO**
Oak	_____	Dove	_____
Tulip	_____	Eagle	_____
Snake	_____	Lizard	_____

Translate the words and put them in the labyrinth.

Traduzca las palabras y páselas al laberinto.

Trees and Flowers ★ Árboles y flores

Translate the English word from **column one** into Spanish. Write the Spanish word in **column two.** Delete the letter indicated in **column three** and add the letter from **column four.** Use the new letters to form a word in Spanish that is equivalent to the English word in **column six.** Write the new word in **column five.** Follow the model.

Traduzca la palabra inglesa de la **primera columna** al español. Escriba la palabra española en la **segunda columna.** Quite la letra indicada en la **tercera columna** y añada la letra de la **cuarta columna.** Use las letras nuevas para hacer una palabra en español que equivale a la palabra inglesa de la **sexta columna.** Escriba la palabra nueva en la **quinta columna.** Siga el modelo.

1 English	2 Spanish	3 –	4 +	5 Spanish	6 English
Model: Twelve	DOCE	D	L	CELO	Zeal
1. Poplar	_____	Á	S	_____	Psalm
2. Maple	_____	R	B	_____	Scholarship
3. Cedar	_____	D	A	_____	Steel
4. Elm	_____	M	S	_____	Alone
5. Palm	_____	M	Y	_____	Beach
6. Pine	_____	N	H	_____	Hiccup
7. Willow	_____	E	A	_____	Reason
8. Lily	_____	O	V	_____	Manly
9. Rose	_____	R	C	_____	Chaos
10. Flowers	_____	L	C	_____	Cool

Section 2
Sección 2

People, Places, and Things
✍ ★ ✍
Gente, lugares y cosas

Getting Dressed ★ Vistiéndose

Handkerchief	_____	Raincoat	_____
Scarf	**BUFANDA**	Necktie	_____
Suit	_____	Cap	_____
Blouse	_____	To clothe	_____
Shirts	_____		

Translate the English words into Spanish. Write the Spanish words in the horizontal spaces. They all pertain to the classification represented by the vertical word.

Traduzca las palabras al español. Escriba las palabras españolas en los espacios horizontales. Todas pertenecen a la clasificación representada por la palabra vertical.

Capitals and Countries ★ Capitales y países

```
A  C  I  R  A  T  S  O  C  V  B  Ú  Y
P  P  A  S  V  Y  A  U  G  A  R  A  P
E  A  Ñ  A  E  U  A  B  U  C  V  I  O
R  N  A  R  N  C  Y  T  C  W  E  É  Y
Ú  I  P  U  E  B  I  H  S  L  M  E  A
Y  T  S  D  Z  O  I  L  S  B  B  E  U
M  N  E  N  U  L  P  A  E  T  R  C  G
P  E  P  O  E  I  L  F  R  B  A  U  A
J  G  Ú  H  L  V  A  Q  Ñ  E  S  A  R
P  R  O  I  A  I  N  V  B  R  I  D  A
E  A  O  D  C  A  I  B  M  O  L  O  C
L  T  O  Y  C  O  C  I  X  É  M  R  I
U  R  U  G  U  A  Y  O  P  K  M  L  N
```

Write the country for each capital city in the list. Look for the countries in the puzzle. They may be situated horizontally, vertically, or diagonally, forward or backward. Draw a circle around each country you find and write an X beside the country in the list.

Escriba el país de cada capital de la lista. Busque los países en la sopa de letras. Pueden situarse horizontal, vertical o diagonalmente, en un sentido o el opuesto. Dibuje un círculo alrededor de cada país que encuentre y escriba una X al lado del país de la lista.

Capital	Country	Capital	Country
La Paz	_____	Asunción	_____
Santiago	_____	San Salvador (2 words)	_____
Managua	_____	Buenos Aires	_____
Lima	**PERÚ**	Bogotá	_____
Montevideo	_____	Habana	_____
Caracas	_____	Madrid	_____
Tegucigalpa	_____	Belmopán	_____
Quito	_____	Brasilia	_____
San José (2 words)	_____	México, D.F.	_____

11

Descriptions ★ Descripciones

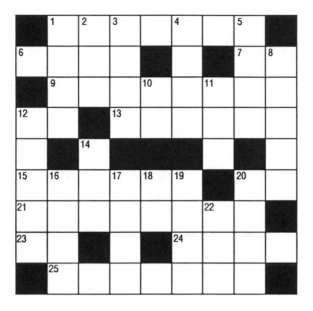

Write the horizontal answers in Spanish and the vertical answers in English.

Escriba las soluciones horizontales en español y las soluciones verticales en inglés.

Horizontal

1. Tired *(fem.)*
6. There
7. Radioactive *(Abbr.)*
9. They applaud
12. Sao Paulo, Brazil *(Abbr.)*
13. They enter
15. They go too far
20. Deciliter *(Abbr.)*
21. Lazy *(fem.)*
23. Already
24. Useful
25. Brunettes

Vertical

1. Aplauda
2. Montaña suiza
3. Río egipcio
4. Lindar con
5. Superficie; región
8. Anular
10. Un
11. Árido
12. Jabonoso
14. Nuestro
16. Rayo
17. Chamuscar
18. Estado de Phoenix *(abrev.)*
19. Sustantivo *(gram.)*
20. Tarima
22. Estación *(abrev.)*

The Beauty Salon ★ El salón de belleza

Translate the words and put them in the labyrinth.

Traduzca las palabras y páselas al laberinto.

Cosmetics	_____	Comb	_____
Mirror	_____	Cream	_____
Red-haired	_____	Freckles	_____
Brush	_____	Massage	_____
File	_____	Braids	_____
Brunette	_____	Nails	**UÑAS**
Powder	_____	Wig	_____
Makeup	_____	Mole	_____

The Human Body ★ El cuerpo humano

Write the horizontal answers in Spanish and the vertical answers in English.

Escriba las soluciones horizontales en español y las soluciones verticales en inglés.

Horizontal	Vertical
1. Palate	1. Poroso
8. Heart	2. Árido
9. To the	3. Más perezoso
10. Nose	4. Phoenix es su capital *(abrev.)*
11. Cream (from milk)	5. Hacer
13. Knees	6. Nombre de una mujer
15. I heard	7. Helado
16. To pose	8. Automóvil
18. Town square	9. A; en
20. Tea	12. Tan
21. Rent *(noun)*	14. Pertenece a los ojos
25. Elbow	15. Onza *(abrev.)*
27. King Tut, now	17. Inglés viejo *(abrev.)*
28. Verb ending	18. Primitivo
29. Summary	19. Enfermedad de la sangre
32. Back *(anat.)*	21. Aviso
	22. Pérdida
	23. Dios; Nuestro Señor
	24. ____ de Janeiro
	26. O
	30. Arriba
	31. Madre

Careers ★ Carreras

```
J   U   N   A   M   T   S   O   P   L   E
Y   T   U   P   R   I   E   S   T   X   R
E   R   R   O   E   R   T   A   M   E   D
G   E   S   A   O   M   I   R   G   S   E
D   K   E   T   N   L   Y   A   E   N   Z
U   R   C   P   O   S   N   L   G   A   L
J   O   U   R   N   A   L   I   S   T   A
D   W   Y   D   M   E   N   A   R   O   W
I   M   I   C   R   E   Y   L   T   X   Y
N   A   M   R   E   H   S   I   F   O   E
M   Y   S   R   E   H   C   A   E   T   R
```

Translate the words into English. Look in the puzzle for the words you have written in the list. They may situated horizontally, vertically, or diagonally, forward or backward. Draw a circle around each word you find and write an X beside the word in the list.

Traduzca las palabras al inglés. Busque en la sopa de letras todas las palabras que haya escrito en la lista. Pueden situarse horizontal, vertical o diagonalmente, en un sentido o el opuesto. Dibuje un círculo alrededor de cada palabra que encuentre y escriba una X al lado de la palabra de la lista.

Abogado	_____	Médico	_____
Cartero	_____	Periodista	_____
Criada	_____	Pescador	_____
Enfermera	_____	Sastre	_____
Gerente	_____	Trabajador	_____
Ingeniero	_____	Traductor	_____
Juez	**JUDGE**	Cura	_____
Maestros	_____	Vendedor	_____

16

Clothing and Footwear ★ La ropa y el calzado

Translate the English word from **column one** into Spanish. Write the Spanish word in **column two**. Delete the letter indicated in **column three** and add the letter from **column four**. Use the new letters to form a word in Spanish that is equivalent to the English word in **column six**. Write the new word in **column five**. Follow the model.

Traduzca la palabra inglesa de la **primera columna** al español. Escriba la palabra española en la **segunda columna**. Quite la letra indicada en la **tercera columna** y añada la letra de la **cuarta columna**. Use las letras nuevas para hacer una palabra en español que equivale a la palabra inglesa de la **sexta columna**. Escriba la palabra nueva en la **quinta columna**. Siga el modelo.

1	2	3	4	5	6
English	**Spanish**	**–**	**+**	**Spanish**	**English**
Model: Twelve	DOCE	D	L	CELO	Zeal
1. Suit	_____	J	S	_____	To be
2. Shoes	_____	P	M	_____	Mustard
3. Sleeve	_____	N	I	_____	Magic
4. Overcoat	_____	G	R	_____	District
5. Cap	_____	R	B	_____	Grace
6. Fabric	_____	T	L	_____	She
7. Lace	_____	J	L	_____	Link
8. Thread	_____	L	J	_____	Son
9. Coat	_____	C	E	_____	Cleanliness
10. Purse	_____	L	R	_____	Sip; gulp
11. Wool	_____	N	B	_____	Bullet
12. Silk	_____	D	M	_____	Table

17

Section 3
Sección 3

Food

★

La comida

At the Restaurant ★ En el restaurante

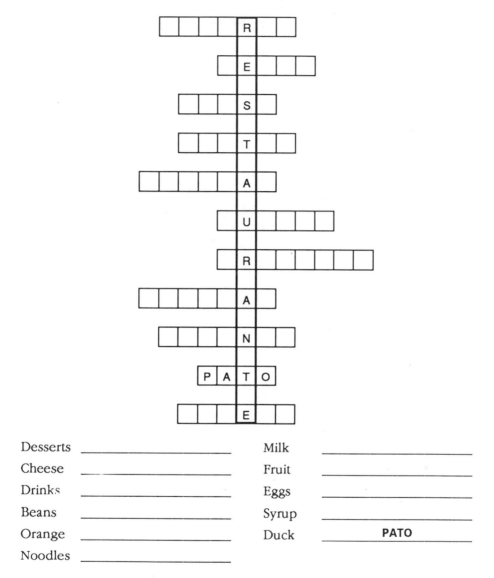

Desserts	_____	Milk	_____
Cheese	_____	Fruit	_____
Drinks	_____	Eggs	_____
Beans	_____	Syrup	_____
Orange	_____	Duck	**PATO**
Noodles	_____		

Translate the English words into Spanish. Write the Spanish words in the horizontal spaces. They all pertain to the classification represented by the vertical word.

Traduzca las palabras inglesas al español. Escriba las palabras españolas en los espacios horizontales. Todas pertenecen a la clasificación representada por la palabra vertical.

Food ★ La comida

```
E  S  E  N  O  R  A  M  A  C  F  A
A  A  B  V  T  S  G  T  R  Ó  C  R
E  L  P  P  S  O  O  A  P  E  K  U
S  O  E  V  D  J  S  P  I  A  I  T
T  D  R  Ó  R  L  Y  T  A  B  E  I
O  L  D  F  A  A  U  J  A  A  O  F
F  A  I  S  Á  N  M  E  R  D  L  N
A  C  Z  D  A  G  C  D  T  E  A  O
D  X  C  S  V  O  I  B  C  J  B  C
O  S  T  R  A  S  A  H  R  O  Ó  I
A  H  C  U  R  T  E  U  L  P  R  R
O  S  E  U  Q  A  O  D  A  N  E  V
```

Translate the words into Spanish. Look in the puzzle for the words you have written in the list. They may be situated horizontally, vertically, or diagonally, forward or backward. Draw a circle around each word you find and write an *X* beside the word in the list.

Traduzca las palabras al español. Busque en la sopa de letras todas las palabras que haya escrito en la lista. Pueden situarse horizontal, vertical o diagonalmente, en un sentido o el opuesto. Dibuje un círculo alrededor de cada palabra que encuentre y escriba una *X* al lado de la palabra de la lista.

Stew	_____	Preserves	_____
Soup	_____	Cheese	_____
Olives	_____	Bass	_____
Pheasant	_____	Milk	_____
Toast	_____	Venison	_____
Codfish	_____	Lobster	_____
Broth	_____	Cider	_____
Oysters	_____	Trout	_____
Salt	**SAL**	Sauce	_____
Partridge	_____	Shrimp	_____

21

Let's Eat! ★ ¡Vamos a comer!

The clues are written in English. Write the answers in Spanish in the puzzle. Note that sometimes a letter has a written accent in the vertical word it belongs to, but not in the horizontal word, or vice versa.

Los indicios están escritos en inglés. Escriba las soluciones en español en el crucigrama. Note que a veces una letra tiene un acento escrito en la palabra vertical en que figura, pero no en la horizontal, o vice versa.

Horizontal

1. Banana
5. It's worth
6. To tie
7. Symmetrical *(abbr.)*
8. Myself
9. Lower California *(abbr.)*
10. Orange
13. He goes
14. To the
15. Garlic
17. Ouch!
18. You love
19. Nor
20. Elbow
21. Frog

Vertical

1. She skates
2. Flame
3. Air *(pref.)*
4. Sidewalk
5. You go
8. Bad
9. Descent
11. Ray
12. Ham
13. They see
16. Bear
18. Here

Scrambled Food ★ La comida revuelta

In the first column are the scrambled letters of words in English and Spanish. In the second column are the Spanish words. Cross out the letters of each Spanish word in the first column. With the remaining letters, form the equivalent word in English. Write the word in the third column. Follow the model.

En la primera columna hay las letras revueltas de palabras en inglés y español. En la segunda columna hay las palabras en español. Tache las letras de cada palabra española en la primera columna. De las letras restantes, forme la palabra equivalente en inglés. Pase la palabra a la tercera columna. Siga el modelo.

Model: MAREÇATEX	CARNE	**MEAT**
1. JORGABRCANCE	CANGREJO	
2. PARBUNTINO	NABO	
3. LLOPICHOCENK	POLLO	
4. REOPYCIELA	APIO	
5. GARÚCARZÚSA	AZUCAR	
6. BONICAONLLEO	CEBOLLA	
7. NAMÓJHMA	JAMÓN	
8. PRAMICSHAMRÓN	CAMARÓN	
9. HÁRBONSADIRA	RÁBANO	
10. ONCIBATOCON	TOCINO	
11. LAVERTENARE	TERNERA	
12. BANDERAP	PAN	
13. BOJERTINBOCA	CONEJO	
14. RAVTYEKUPO	PAVO	
15. ESHUCEQEOSE	QUESO	
16. NARZÍMOC	MAÍZ	
17. OUTTARCHURT	TRUCHA	
18. ROPUCKERPO	PUERCO	
19. CAPUKODT	PATO	
20. CORZIRARE	ARROZ	

Vegetables ★ Verduras

Translate the words and put them in the labyrinth.

Traduzca las palabras y páselas al laberinto.

Cucumber	_____	Celery	**APIO**
Artichoke	_____	Radish	_____
Pumpkin	_____	Lettuce	_____
Onion	_____	Turnip	_____
Rice	_____	Beans	_____
Watercress	_____	Cabbage	_____
Mushrooms	_____	Carrot	_____
Chickpea	_____	Sweet potato	_____

Vegetables and Fruit ★ Verduras y frutas

Translate the English word from **column one** into Spanish. Write the Spanish word in **column two**. Delete the letter indicated in **column three** and add the letter from **column four**. Use the new letters to form a word in Spanish that is equivalent to the English word in **column six**. Write the new word in **column five**. Follow the model.

Traduzca la palabra inglesa de la **primera columna** al español. Escriba la palabra española en la **segunda columna**. Quite la letra indicada en la **tercera columna** y añada la letra de la **cuarta columna**. Use las letras nuevas para hacer una palabra en español que equivale a la palabra inglesa de la **sexta columna**. Escriba la palabra nueva en la **quinta columna**. Siga el modelo.

1 English	2 Spanish	3 −	4 +	5 Spanish	6 English
Model: Twelve	DOCE	D	L	CELO	Zeal
1. Celery		A	S		Floor
2. Rice		R	M		March
3. Cabbage		C	S		The (m. pl.)
4. Corn		M	R		Root
5. Turnip		B	Z		Ounce
6. Onion		C	T		Bottle
7. Potato		P	S		Raisin
8. Cucumber		P	S		Thornbush
9. Mushroom		G	D		Deep
10. Watercress		B	P		Dog
11. Cherry		C	P		Laziness
12. Pear		P	Z		Prays

Section 4
Sección 4

Language
★
El lenguaje

Language ★ El lenguaje

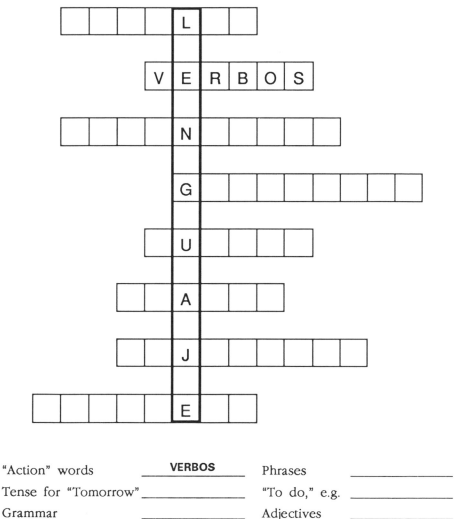

"Action" words   **VERBOS**   Phrases   _____

Tense for "Tomorrow"_____   "To do," e.g. _____

Grammar   _____   Adjectives   _____

The ABCs   _____   A, E, I, O, U _____

Translate the English words into Spanish. Write the Spanish words in the horizontal spaces. They all pertain to the classification represented by the vertical word.

Traduzca las palabras inglesas al español. Escriba las palabras españolas en los espacios horizontales. Todas pertenecen a la clasificación representada por la palabra vertical.

Verbs ★ Verbos

Write the verbs in Spanish in the two forms indicated. Look for the verb forms in the puzzle. They may be situated horizontally, vertically, or diagonally, forward or backward. Draw a circle around each word you find and write an X beside the word in the list.

Escriba los verbos en español en las dos formas indicadas. Busque las formas en la sopa de letras. Pueden situarse horizontal, vertical o diagonalmente, en un sentido o el opuesto. Dibuje un círculo alrededor de cada palabra que encuentre y escriba una X al lado de la palabra de la lista.

English	Infinitive	Present Tense (Yo)	Past (Preterite) Tense (Yo)
1. Be	_____		_____
2. Go		_____	_____
3. Prove	_____	_____	
4. Want		_____	_____
5. Seek	_____		_____
6. Fall	**CAER**	_____	
7. Count		_____	_____
8. Say	_____	_____	
9. Play	_____	_____	
10. Hear		_____	_____
11. Smell		_____	_____
12. Place		_____	_____
13. Know	_____		_____
14. Have	_____		_____

```
O  H  J  A  Í  E  O  Q  U  I  S  E  E
B  U  P  L  É  Y  Í  V  R  E  B  A  S
E  E  Í  F  Q  T  P  O  N  G  O  S  T
U  L  J  U  G  A  R  E  G  O  L  Í  U
R  O  A  I  Z  I  O  G  I  D  S  E  V
P  É  U  Q  S  U  B  É  T  N  O  C  E
O  J  D  A  Q  Í  A  U  P  L  A  U  B
N  U  E  S  T  A  R  S  Q  I  B  E  U
G  E  C  A  S  L  D  C  G  B  V  N  S
O  G  I  O  M  P  N  O  B  O  V  T  C
Z  O  R  J  T  U  V  E  Y  U  Q  O  A
S  U  P  E  Z  S  Y  Q  T  E  N  E  R
É  Q  Y  C  A  E  R  O  R  E  I  U  Q
```

Past Participles ★ Los participios

In the first column are the scrambled letters of words in English and Spanish. In the second column are the English words. Cross out the letters of each English word in the first column. With the remaining letters, form the past participle of that word in Spanish. Write the participle in the third column. Follow the model.

En la primera columna hay las letras revueltas de palabras en inglés y español. En la segunda columna hay las palabras en inglés. Tache las letras de cada palabra inglesa en la primera columna. De las letras restantes, forme el participio de esa palabra en español. Pase el participio a la tercera columna. Siga el modelo.

Model: COYDJSHA	SAY	**DICHO**
1. SACKEBODUSE	SEEK	
2. ROPINEABOTE	OPEN	
3. GADIRTISOTA	STIR	
4. DANKOWALAD	WALK	
5. MOSKAFUMEDO	SMOKE	
6. SAROMYCADAR	MARRY	
7. JOLAREWOBAD	LOWER	
8. TAGINOBRÍRD	BRING	
9. DOVALOMEA	LOVE	
10. ZONEJADYOGO	ENJOY	
11. MACOTIDEO	EAT	
12. WECIRSITTERO	WRITE	
13. CESAHIDUPEO	ESCAPE	
14. LÍFOALDAC	FALL	
15. EDAVILESALO	LEAVE	
16. GUDALPOJAY	PLAY	
17. KINBEDRIDOB	DRINK	
18. VASOWALHAD	WASH	
19. PADOYALHUDE	HELP	
20. RUDYMABOPOC	BUY	

Relative Pronouns and Other Words ★ Pronombres relativos y otras palabras

Translate the words and put them in the labyrinth.

Traduzca las palabras y páselas al laberinto.

When?	_____	Never (#1)	_____
Because	_____	Never (#2)	_____
Where?	_____	Nobody	_____
Who	_____	Nothing	_____
As, like	_____	None	_____
That	_____	Neither	_____
Which	_____	No	**NO**

Adjectives ★ Adjetivos

Write the horizontal answers in Spanish and the vertical answers in English.

Escriba las soluciones horizontales en español y las soluciones verticales en inglés.

Horizontal	Vertical
1. Vacant *(pl.)*	1. Apodo de Daniel
7. I love	2. Surgir
8. Negative	3. Sociología
9. Essential	4. Estados Unidos
15. Rhyme	5. Sobre
16. Bridegroom	6. Único
17. Self	10. Mercado del Europa *(abrev.)*
18. My	11. Mismo
19. Tea	12. Enfermera *(abrev.)*
20. He rereads	13. Cantidad muy pequeña
21. Caterpillar, e.g.	14. Encima de
23. It	17. Terminación comparativa
24. Black *(f.)*	21. Juega al tenis
25. It bubbled *(preterite)*	22. Terciopelo
27. Plural ending	24. Nombre
29. Thrilling	26. A
	27. En
	28. Sudeste *(abrev.)*

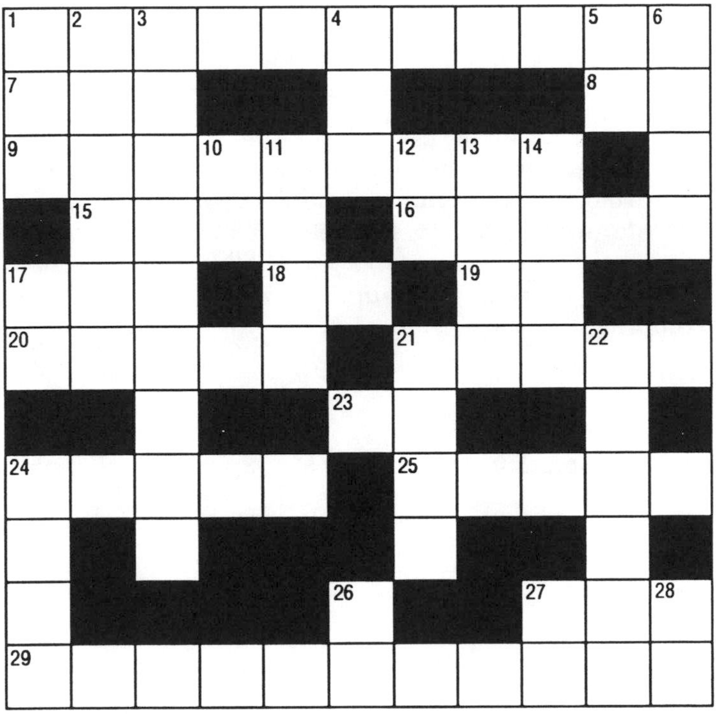
1
2
3
4
5
6
7
8
9
10
11
12
13
14
15
16
17
18
19
20
21
22
23
24
25
26
27
28
29

Infinitives ★ Infinitivos

Translate the English word from **column one** into Spanish. Write the Spanish word in **column two.** Delete the letter indicated in **column three** and add the letter from **column four.** Use the new letters to form a word in Spanish that is equivalent to the English word in **column six.** Write the new word in **column five.** Follow the model.

Traduzca la palabra inglesa de la **primera columna** al español. Escriba la palabra española en la **segunda columna.** Quite la letra indicada en la **tercera columna** y añada la letra de la **cuarta columna.** Use las letras nuevas para hacer una palabra en español que equivale a la palabra inglesa de la **sexta columna.** Escriba la palabra nueva en la **quinta columna.** Siga el modelo.

1 English	2 Spanish	3 −	4 +	5 Spanish	6 English
Model: Twelve	DOCE	D	L	CELO	Zeal
1. To eat	_____	C	T	_____	Meter
2. To fall	_____	R	J	_____	Eyebrow
3. To use	_____	U	T	_____	After
4. To read	_____	R	V	_____	Light
5. To bind	_____	T	S	_____	To roast
6. To dare	_____	R	E	_____	Cleanliness
7. To smell	_____	L	C	_____	Zero
8. To flee	_____	H	N	_____	To unite
9. To scratch	_____	Y	J	_____	To split
10. To erase	_____	R	T	_____	To sprout
11. To love	_____	M	P	_____	For
12. To hear	_____	O	A	_____	Estuary

Section 5
Sección 5

Daily Life
✍ ★ ✍
La vida cotidiana

Families ★ Familias

Granddaughter	____________	Stepfather	____________
Sister	____________	Great grandfather	____________
Nephew	____________	Godson	____________
Brotherly	FRATERNAL	Grandmother	____________

Translate the English words into Spanish. Write the Spanish words in the horizontal spaces. They all pertain to the classification represented by the vertical word.

Traduzca las palabras inglesas al español. Escriba las palabras españolas en los espacios horizontales. Todas pertenecen a la clasificación representada por la palabra vertical.

The Family ★ La familia

Translate the words and put them in the labyrinth.

Traduzca las palabras y páselas al laberinto.

Sister	_____	Cook	_____
Child	_____	Uncle	_____ TÍO _____
Nursemaid	_____	Servant	_____
Mother	_____	Grandfather	_____
Gardener	_____	Cousin	_____
Maid	_____		

At the Hospital ★ En el hospital

```
J  S  C  O  S  T  I  L  L  A  S  J
P  O  C  Y  O  A  E  S  A  N  E  V
V  T  A  Í  S  U  R  Ó  T  R  G  Á
E  E  R  Ñ  A  U  É  I  I  O  P  A
N  L  D  C  P  D  T  N  P  O  I  R
D  E  Í  O  A  A  G  U  C  S  I  E
A  U  A  R  C  A  C  I  R  Ñ  E  M
J  Q  C  A  R  Y  D  I  Ó  A  O  R
E  S  O  Z  A  É  M  N  E  Z  S  E
S  E  N  Ó  M  L  U  P  A  N  K  F
P  O  E  N  Á  R  C  B  V  U  T  N
P  A  L  L  I  L  B  A  T  Y  E  E
```

Translate the words into Spanish. Look in the puzzle for the words you have written in the list. They may be situated horizontally, vertically, or diagonally, forward or backward. Draw a circle around each word you find and write an X beside the word in the list.

Traduzca las palabras al español. Busque en la sopa de letras todas las palabras que haya escrito en la lista. Pueden situarse horizontal, vertical o diagonalmente, en un sentido o el opuesto. Dibuje un círculo alrededor de cada palabra que encuentre y escriba una X al lado de la palabra de la lista.

Bandages	_____	Lung	_____
Splint	_____	Heart	_____
Patient	_____	Spleen	**BAZO**
Breathe	_____	Kidney	_____
Syringe	_____	Veins	_____
Doctor	_____	Skeleton	_____
Pacemakers	_____	Ribs	_____
Of the heart	_____	Nurse	_____
Sutures	_____	Skull	_____

Time and Weather ★ La hora y el tiempo

In the first column are the scrambled letters of words in English and Spanish. In the second column are the English words. Cross out the letters of each English word in the first column. With the remaining letters, form the equivalent word in Spanish. Write the word in the third column. Follow the model.

En la primera columna hay las letras revueltas de palabras en inglés y español. En la segunda columna hay las palabras en inglés. Tache las letras de cada palabra inglesa en la primera columna. De las letras restantes, forme la palabra equivalente en español. Pase la palabra a la tercera columna. Siga el modelo.

Model: H̶O̶N̶A̶M̶N̶A̶D̶	HAND	MANO
1. GONETHINCH	NIGHT	
2. TILGYERCUNOS	CENTURY	
3. VIARUNILLA	RAIN	
4. ADEFATECH	DATE	
5. ILOCEHIE	ICE	
6. JOLCELKORC	CLOCK	
7. DULBENUCO	CLOUD	
8. ALIRADYIDIO	DAILY	
9. FACHORCARSTES	FROST	
10. MEPOTIMEIT	TIME	
11. GIEFOBALN	FOG	
12. WORÍCEDO	DEW	
13. NSHEMOTM	MONTH	
14. DEWIVONTIN	WIND	
15. LORCÍFOD	COLD	
16. WENOVISEN	SNOW	
17. RAYOÑEA	YEAR	
18. HARBEDSAMOS	SHADE	
19. DRONTEHURNUTE	THUNDER	
20. KAMEWENASE	WEEK	

41

At the Table ★ En la mesa

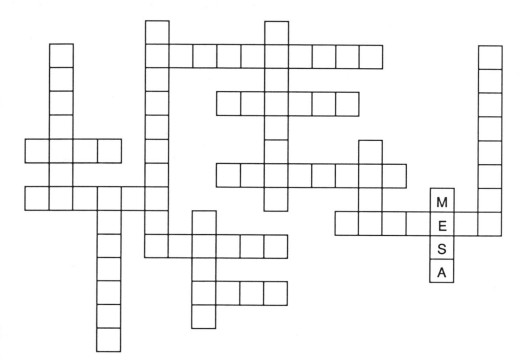

Translate the words and put them in the labyrinth.

Traduzca las palabras y páselas al laberinto.

Napkin	_____	Saltshaker	_____
Saucer	_____	Teapot	_____
Bowls	_____	Table	**MESA**
Spoon	_____	Plate	_____
Goblet	_____	Tray	_____
Tablecloth	_____	Fork	_____
Toothpicks	_____	Cup	_____
Glass	_____	Coffeepot	_____

The Home ★ La casa

Translate the English word from **column one** into Spanish. Write the Spanish word in **column two.** Delete the letter indicated in **column three** and add the letter from **column four.** Use the new letters to form a word in Spanish that is equivalent to the English word in **column six.** Write the new word in **column five.** Follow the model.

Traduzca la palabra inglesa de la **primera columna** al español. Escriba la palabra española en la **segunda columna.** Quite la letra indicada en la **tercera columna** y añada la letra de la **cuarta columna.** Use las letras nuevas para hacer una palabra en español que equivale a la palabra inglesa de la **sexta columna.** Escriba la palabra nueva en la **quinta columna.** Siga el modelo.

1 English	2 Spanish	3 −	4 +	5 Spanish	6 English
Model: Twelve	DOCE	D	L	CELO	Zeal
1. Mirror		J	S		Thick
2. Bed		M	V		Cow
3. Table		E	A		Dough
4. Bath		B	D		Harm
5. Tub		I	A		Cream
6. House		C	L		Living room
7. Floor		I	E		Mexican money
8. Clock		L	Z		Redness
9. Chair		S	V		Small town
10. AM/FM		I	B		Bard
11. Courtyard		I	S		Grass
12. Balcony		B	H		Falcon

Section 6
Sección 6

Recreation and Sports
★
El recreo y los deportes

Recreation ★ El recreo

		P				

C	A	N	C	H	A	S

Swords (fencing) _____

Games (soccer) _____

Playing cards _____

Tennis equipment _____

Billiard cues _____

Gym _____

Bullfight _____

Tennis courts __**CANCHAS**__

Bowling balls _____

Skis _____

Swimming pool _____

Translate the English words into Spanish. Write the Spanish words in the horizontal spaces. They all pertain to the classification represented by the vertical word.

Traduzca las palabras inglesas al español. Escriba las palabras españolas en los espacios horizontales. Todas pertenecen a la clasificación representada por la palabra vertical.

47

Buildings and Arenas ★ Edificios y ruedos

Translate the words into Spanish. Look in the puzzle for the words you have written in the list. They may be situated horizontally, vertically, or diagonally, forward or backward. Draw a circle around each word you find and write an *X* beside the word in the list.

Traduzca las palabras al español. Busque en la sopa de letras todas las palabras que haya escrito en la lista. Pueden situarse horizontal, vertical or diagonalmente, en un sentido o el opuesto. Dibuje un círculo alrededor de cada palabra que encuentre y escriba una *X* al lado de la palabra de la lista.

Post office	_____	Museum	_____
Medical building	_____	Academy	_____
Wine cellar/shop	_____	Town square	_____
Library	_____	Coffee shop	**CAFÉ**
Arena	_____	Customs	_____
Barn	_____	Warehouse	_____
Movie theater	_____	Asylum	_____
School	_____	House	_____
Store	_____	Jai alai court	_____
Bullfight	_____	Stationery shop	_____
Bank	_____	Workshop	_____

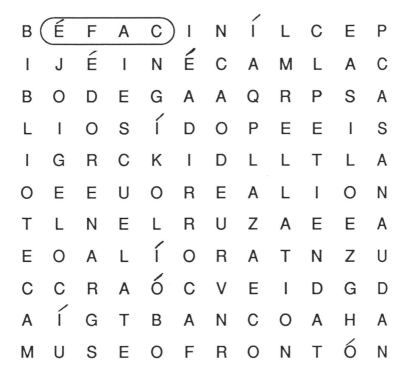

```
B  É  F  A  C  I  N  Í  L  C  E  P
I  J  É  I  N  É  C  A  M  L  A  C
B  O  D  E  G  A  A  Q  R  P  S  A
L  I  O  S  Í  D  O  P  E  E  I  S
I  G  R  C  K  I  D  L  L  T  L  A
O  E  E  U  O  R  E  A  L  I  O  N
T  L  N  E  L  R  U  Z  A  E  E  A
E  O  A  L  Í  O  R  A  T  N  Z  U
C  C  R  A  Ó  C  V  E  I  D  G  D
A  Í  G  T  B  A  N  C  O  A  H  A
M  U  S  E  O  F  R  O  N  T  Ó  N
```

49

Amusement ★ Diversiones

In the first column are the scrambled letters of words in English and Spanish. In the second column are the English words. Cross out the letters of each English word in the first column. With the remaining letters, form the equivalent word in Spanish. Write the word in the third column. Follow the model.

En la primera columna hay las letras revueltas de palabras en inglés y español. En la segunda columna hay las palabras en inglés. Tache las letras de cada palabra inglesa en la primera columna. De las letras restantes, forme la palabra equivalente en español. Pase la palabra a la tercera columna. Siga el modelo.

Model: ~~NISTESIN~~ENT	TENNIS	TENIS
1. RAFITYSEPAT	PARTY	
2. SHERZEAJSEDC	CHESS	
3. IROCELUISEO	LEISURE	
4. LAVEJIRAVATR	(To) TRAVEL	
5. MAJOSEGUSEG	GAMES	
6. SACHIGEPSNIF	FISHING	
7. DAWIRAMNS	(To) SWIM	
8. KUISEQÍS	SKI	
9. LABECINADE	DANCE	
10. EVONCIMIE	MOVIE	
11. CROSCIRCUCI	CIRCUS	
12. GUNZATHINAC	HUNTING	
13. BÓFINCHIBOYA	HOBBY	
14. RAFAIRFIE	FAIR	
15. NATEKSAPIRAT	(To) SKATE	
16. JILBOKSACECH	JACKS	
17. PANSERCAIDS	CARDS	
18. TÓLBALNOFOLAB	FOOTBALL	
19. SERDOPTOPERT	SPORT	
20. EFARDELISDAPE	PARADE	

Leisure Time ★ Tiempo libre

Write the horizontal answers in Spanish and the vertical answers in English.

Escriba las soluciones horizontales en español y las soluciones verticales en inglés.

Horizontal

1. Chess
7. Tilt
8. Or
10. Nine-inning game
13. He is
15. U.S.A.
16. I see
18. Telephone *(abbr.)*
19. April *(abbr.)*
22. Bullfight
26. In
27. Dry
29. Fencing

Vertical

1. Décimosexto presidente, E.U. *(iniciales)*
2. Puñetazo en boxeo
3. Paraíso
4. Divinidad
5. Desfile famoso en Pasadena
6. Colección de animales salvajes
9. Dispositivo
11. Pero
12. Lila
14. Sudeste *(abrev.)*
20. Jactarse
21. Mil quinientos y dos *(rom.)*
23. Uno
24. Irregular *(abrev.)*
25. Almirante *(abrev.)*
28. Oficina del almirante *(abrev.)*

Having Fun ★ Divirtiéndose

Translate the English word from **column one** into Spanish. Write the Spanish word in **column two**. Delete the letter indicated in **column three** and add the letter from **column four**. Use the new letters to form a word in Spanish that is equivalent to the English word in **column six**. Write the new word in **column five**. Follow the model.

Traduzca la palabra inglesa de la **primera columna** al español. Escriba la palabra española en la **segunda columna.** Quite la letra indicada en la **tercera columna** y añada la letra de la **cuarta columna.** Use las letras nuevas para hacer una palabra en español que equivale a la palabra inglesa de la **sexta columna.** Escriba la palabra nueva en la **quinta columna.** Siga el modelo.

1	2	3	4	5	6
English	**Spanish**	**–**	**+**	**Spanish**	**English**
Model: Twelve	DOCE	D	L	CELO	Zeal
1. Leisure	_____	C	G	_____	I hear
2. Bat (baseball)	_____	B	M	_____	Theme
3. Art	_____	E	A	_____	Rat
4. Hunting	_____	Z	R	_____	Face
5. Movie theater	_____	C	B	_____	Well
6. Court (tennis)	_____	A	O	_____	Shell
7. To read	_____	R	V	_____	Light (weight)
8. Track	_____	S	R	_____	To whistle
9. Dance	_____	E	R	_____	April
10. Circus	_____	R .	N	_____	Five
11. To swim	_____	R	Z	_____	Dancing
12. Boat	_____	R	N	_____	Bank

Answers
Soluciones

✍ ★ ✍

✏ 1 ✏

Labyrinth / Laberinto

Plants and Animals ★ Plantas y animales

Swallow, GOLONDRINA; Pansy, PENSAMIENTO; Crow, CUERVO, Daisy, MARGARITA; Elephant, ELEFANTE; Pheasant, FAISÁN; Poplar, ÁLAMO; Willow, SAUCE; Horse, CABALLO; Carnation, CLAVEL.

Word Search / Buscapalabras

Birds and Animals ★ Aves y animales

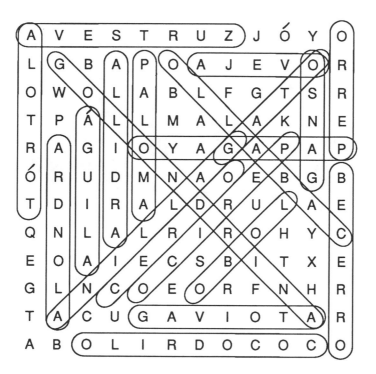

Horse	CABALLO	Sea gull	GAVIOTA
Pig	CERDO	Ostrich	AVESTRUZ
Squirrel	ARDILLA	Swallow	GOLONDRINA
Wolf	LOBO	Turtledove	TÓRTOLA
Crocodile	COCODRILO	Cat	GATO
Calf	BECERRO	Parrot	PAPAGAYO
Sheep	OVEJA	Eagle	ÁGUILA
Hen	GALLINA	Goose	GANSO
Dove	PALOMA	Dog	PERRO
Lark	ALONDRA	Parakeet	PERICO

Bilingual Crossword / Crucigrama bilingüe

More Birds and Animals ★ Más aves y animales

¹E	²A	³G	⁴L	E		⁵H	⁶O	⁷G

Grid:

¹E	²A	³G	⁴L	E	▓	⁵H	⁶O	⁷G
N	▓	⁸O	I	L	▓	⁹E	G	O
¹⁰D	¹¹O	N	K	E	Y	▓	¹²L	A
¹³S	H	E	E	P	▓	¹⁴P	E	T
▓	▓	▓	¹⁵S	H	¹⁶E	▓	▓	▓
¹⁷D	¹⁸O	G	▓	¹⁹A	I	²⁰D	²¹E	²²D
²³O	K	▓	²⁴A	N	G	O	R	A
²⁵E	L	²⁶M	▓	²⁷T	H	E	▓	R
²⁸S	A	Y	▓	²⁹S	T	R	U	T

Bilingual Anagrams / Anagramas bilingües

Scrambled Flora and Fauna ★ Flora y fauna revueltas

1.	APLYOAPOAPMP	POPPY	AMAPOLA
2.	UBSOPAURELLCOD	ROSEBUD	CAPULLO
3.	BABJEINTORCO	RABBIT	CONEJO
4.	FRAZOXOR	FOX	ZORRA
5.	RASOBEO	BEAR	OSO
6.	EJAPEOVESH	SHEEP	OVEJA
7.	WACCOVA	COW	VACA
8.	ELACYEABBARD	BARLEY	CEBADA
9.	ZOMARÍNC	CORN	MAÍZ
10.	MADVAOPELO	DOVE	PALOMA
11.	GONTALOCODÓNT	COTTON	ALGODÓN
12.	ILÁGULEAGEA	EAGLE	ÁGUILA
13.	GIAFIUGHER	FIG (TREE)	HIGUERA
14.	SEACHOORBALL	HORSE	CABALLO
15.	GLOWLANTAUN	WALNUT (TREE)	NOGAL
16.	BALGOCCEBA	CABBAGE	COL
17.	VAPTOKERUY	TURKEY	PAVO
18.	TIARSADGARIAMY	DAISY	MARGARITA
19.	LORPOTRARO	PARROT	LORO
20.	ISPSNORBTAUN	TURNIPS	NABOS

Labyrinth / Laberinto
Nature ★ La naturaleza

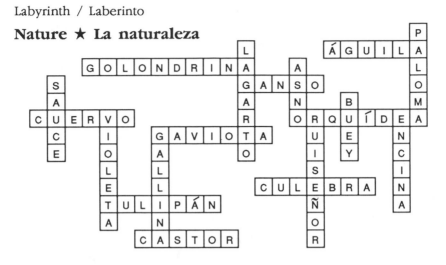

Swallow, GOLONDRINA; Violet, VIOLETA; Beaver, CASTOR; Goose, GANSO; Orchid, ORQUÍDEA; Gull, GAVIOTA; Oak, ENCINA; Tulip, TULIPÁN; Snake, CULEBRA; Willow, SAUCE; Ox, BUEY; Nightingale, RUISEÑOR; Hen, GALLINA; Crow, CUERVO; Donkey, ASNO; Dove, PALOMA; Eagle, ÁGUILA; Lizard, LAGARTO.

Drop and Add / Quite y añada
Trees and Flowers ★ Árboles y flores

1 English	2 Spanish	3 −	4 +	5 Spanish	6 English
1. Poplar	ÁLAMO	Á	S	SALMO	Psalm
2. Maple	ARCE	R	B	BECA	Scholarship
3. Cedar	CEDRO	D	A	ACERO	Steel
4. Elm	OLMO	M	S	SOLO	Alone
5. Palm	PALMA	M	Y	PLAYA	Beach
6. Pine	PINO	N	H	HIPO	Hiccup
7. Willow	SAUCE	E	A	CAUSA	Reason
8. Lily	LIRIO	O	V	VIRIL	Manly
9. Rose	ROSA	R	C	CAOS	Chaos
10. Flowers	FLORES	L	C	FRESCO	Cool

✍ **2** ✍

Word Cross / Palabras cruzadas

Getting Dressed ★ Vistiéndose

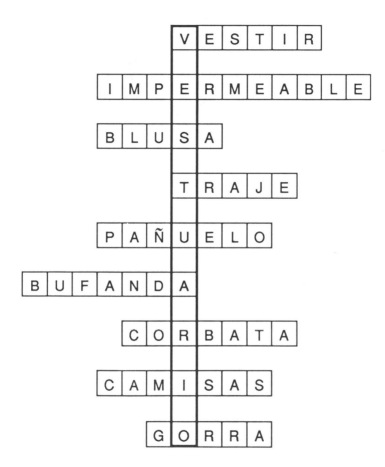

Handkerchief, PAÑUELO; Scarf, BUFANDA; Suit, TRAJE; Blouse, BLUSA; Shirts, CAMISAS; Raincoat, IMPERMEABLE; Necktie, CORBATA; Cap, GORRA; To clothe, VESTIR.

Word Search / Buscapalabras

Capitals and Countries ★ Capitales y países

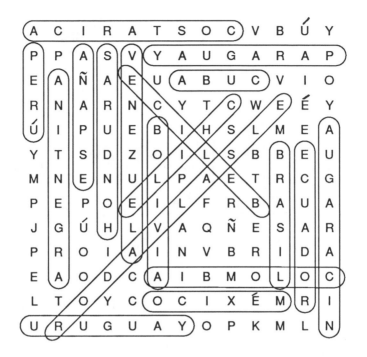

Capital	Country	Capital	Country
La Paz	**BOLIVIA**	Asunción	**PARAGUAY**
Santiago	**CHILE**	San Salvador (2 words)	**EL SALVADOR**
Managua	**NICARAGUA**	Buenos Aires	**ARGENTINA**
Lima	**PERÚ**	Bogotá	**COLOMBIA**
Montevideo	**URUGUAY**	Habana	**CUBA**
Caracas	**VENEZUELA**	Madrid	**ESPAÑA**
Tegucigalpa	**HONDURAS**	Belmopán	**BELICE**
Quito	**ECUADOR**	Brasilia	**BRASIL**
San José (2 words)	**COSTA RICA**	México, D.F.	**MÉXICO**

Bilingual Crossword / Crucigrama bilingüe

Descriptions ★ Descripciones

Labyrinth / Laberinto

The Beauty Salon ★ El salón de belleza

Cosmetics, COSMÉTICOS; Mirror, ESPEJO; Red-haired, PELIRROJO; Brush, CEPILLO; File, LIMA; Brunette, MORENA; Powder, POLVOS; Makeup, MAQUILLAJE; Comb, PEINE; Cream, CREMA; Freckles, PECAS; Massage, MASAJE; Braids, TRENZAS; Nails, UÑAS; Wig, PELUCA; Mole, LUNAR.

Bilingual Crossword / Crucigrama bilingüe

The Human Body ★ El cuerpo humano

		¹P	²A	³L	⁴A	⁵D	⁶A	R		⁷G
	⁸C	O	R	A	Z	O	N		⁹A	L
¹⁰N	A	R	I	Z			¹¹N	¹²A	T	A
	¹³R	O	D	I	L	L	A	S		C
¹⁴O		U		E				¹⁵O	I	
¹⁶P	¹⁷O	S	A	R		¹⁸P	L	¹⁹A	Z	A
²⁰T	E					R		N		L
I		²¹A	²²L	Q	U	I	²³L	E	²⁴R	
²⁵C	²⁶O	D	O			²⁷M	O	M	I	A
²⁸A	R		²⁹S	³⁰U	³¹M	A	R	I	O	
L		³²E	S	P	A	L	D	A		

62

Word Search / Buscapalabras

Careers ★ Carreras

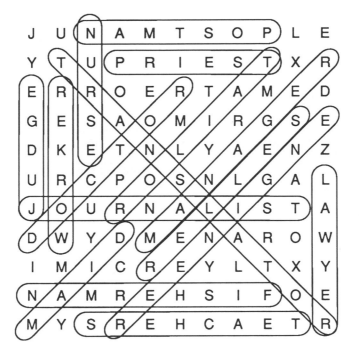

Abogado	LAWYER	Médico	DOCTOR
Cartero	POSTMAN	Periodista	JOURNALIST
Criada	MAID	Pescador	FISHERMAN
Enfermera	NURSE	Sastre	TAILOR
Gerente	MANAGER	Trabajador	WORKER
Ingeniero	ENGINEER	Traductor	TRANSLATOR
Juez	JUDGE	Cura	PRIEST
Maestros	TEACHERS	Vendedor	SELLER

Drop and Add / Quite y añada

Clothing and Footwear ★ La ropa y el calzado

1 English	2 Spanish	3 –	4 +	5 Spanish	6 English
1. Suit	TRAJE	J	S	ESTAR	To be
2. Shoes	ZAPATOS	P	M	MOSTAZA	Mustard
3. Sleeve	MANGA	N	I	MAGIA	Magic
4. Overcoat	ABRIGO	G	R	BARRIO	District
5. Cap	GORRA	R	B	GARBO	Grace
6. Fabric	TELA	T	L	ELLA	She
7. Lace	ENCAJE	J	L	ENLACE	Link
8. Thread	HILO	L	J	HIJO	Son
9. Coat	SACO	C	E	ASEO	Cleanliness
10. Purse	BOLSO	L	R	SORBO	Sip; gulp
11. Wool	LANA	N	B	BALA	Bullet
12. Silk	SEDA	D	M	MESA	Table

3

Word Cross / Palabras cruzadas

At the Restaurant ★ En el restaurante

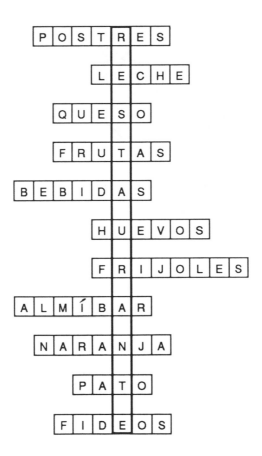

Desserts, POSTRES; Cheese, QUESO; Drinks, BEBIDAS; Beans, FRIJOLES; Orange, NARANJA; Noodles, FIDEOS; Milk, LECHE; Fruit, FRUTAS; Eggs, HUEVOS; Syrup, ALMÍBAR; Duck, PATO.

Word Search / Buscapalabras
Food ★ La comida

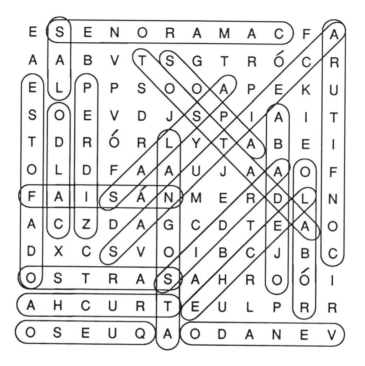

Stew	ESTOFADO	Preserves	CONFITURA
Soup	SOPA	Cheese	QUESO
Olives	ACEITUNAS	Bass	RÓBALO
Pheasant	FAISÁN	Milk	LECHE
Toast	TOSTADA	Venison	VENADO
Codfish	ABADEJO	Lobster	LANGOSTA
Broth	CALDO	Cider	SIDRA
Oysters	OSTRAS	Trout	TRUCHA
Salt	SAL	Sauce	SALSA
Partridge	PERDIZ	Shrimp	CAMARONES

Bilingual Crossword / Crucigrama bilingüe

Let's Eat! ★ ¡Vamos a comer!

Bilingual Anagrams / Anagramas bilingües

Scrambled Food ★ La comida revuelta

1.	JORGABRCANCE	CANGREJO	CRAB
2.	PARBUNTINO	NABO	TURNIP
3.	LLOPICHOCENK	POLLO	CHICKEN
4.	REOPYCIELA	APIO	CELERY
5.	GARÚCARZUSA	AZÚCAR	SUGAR
6.	BONICAONLLEO	CEBOLLA	ONION
7.	NAMÓJHMA	JAMÓN	HAM
8.	PRAMICSHAMRÓN	CAMARÓN	SHRIMP
9.	HÁRBONSADIRA	RÁBANO	RADISH
10.	ONCIBATOCON	TOCINO	BACON
11.	LAVERTENARE	TERNERA	VEAL
12.	BANDERAP	PAN	BREAD
13.	BOJERTINBOCA	CONEJO	RABBIT
14.	RAVTYEKUPO	PAVO	TURKEY
15.	ESHUCEQEOSE	QUESO	CHEESE
16.	NARZÍMOC	MAÍZ	CORN
17.	OUTTARCHURT	TRUCHA	TROUT
18.	ROPUCKERPO	PUERCO	PORK
19.	CAPUKODT	PATO	DUCK
20.	CORZIRARE	ARROZ	RICE

Labyrinth / Laberinto

Vegetables ★ Verduras

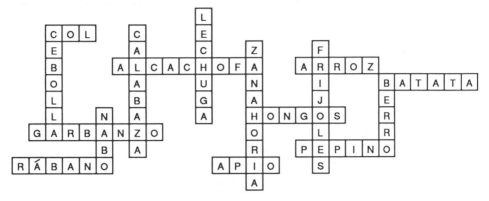

Cucumber, PEPINO; Artichoke, ALCACHOFA; Pumpkin, CALABAZA; Onion, CEBOLLA; Rice, ARROZ; Watercress, BERRO; Mushrooms, HONGOS; Chickpea, GARBANZO; Celery, APIO; Radish, RÁBANO; Lettuce, LECHUGA; Turnip, NABO; Beans, FRIJOLES; Cabbage, COL; Carrot, ZANAHORIA; Sweet Potato, BATATA.

Drop and Add / Quite y añada

Vegetables and Fruit ★ Verduras y frutas

1 English	2 Spanish	3 −	4 +	5 Spanish	6 English
1. Celery	APIO	A	S	PISO	Floor
2. Rice	ARROZ	R	M	MARZO	March
3. Cabbage	COL	C	S	LOS	The *(m. pl.)*
4. Corn	MAÍZ	M	R	RAÍZ	Root
5. Turnip	NABO	B	Z	ONZA	Ounce
6. Onion	CEBOLLA	C	T	BOTELLA	Bottle
7. Potato	PAPA	P	S	PASA	Raisin
8. Cucumber	PEPINO	P	S	ESPINO	Thornbush
9. Mushroom	HONGO	G	D	HONDO	Deep
10. Watercress	BERRO	B	P	PERRO	Dog
11. Cherry	CEREZA	C	P	PEREZA	Laziness
12. Pear	PERA	P	Z	REZA	Prays

$\mathscr{L}$ **4** $\mathscr{L}$

Word Cross / Palabras cruzadas

Language ★ El lenguaje

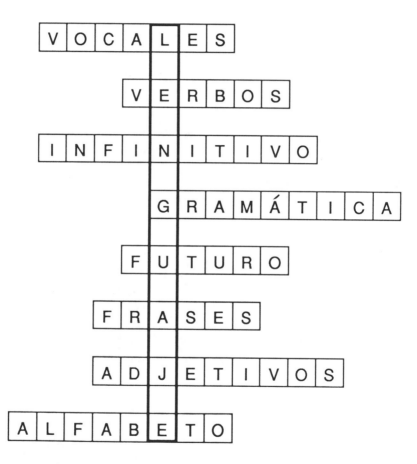

"Action" words, VERBOS; Tense for "tomorrow," FUTURO; Grammar, GRAMÁTICA; The ABCs, ALFABETO; Phrases, FRASES; "To do," e.g., INFINITIVO; Adjectives, ADJETIVOS; A, E, I, O, U, VOCALES.

Word Search / Buscapalabras

Verbs ★ Verbos

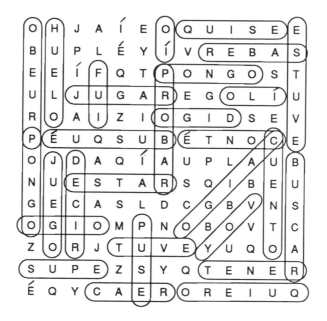

English	Infinitive	Present Tense (Yo)	Past (Preterite) Tense (Yo)
1. Be	ESTAR		ESTUVE
2. Go		VOY	FUI
3. Prove	PROBAR	PRUEBO	
4. Want		QUIERO	QUISE
5. Seek	BUSCAR		BUSQUÉ
6. Fall	CAER	CAIGO	
7. Count		CUENTO	CONTÉ
8. Say	DECIR	DIGO	
9. Play	JUGAR	JUEGO	
10. Hear		OIGO	OÍ
11. Smell		HUELO	OLÍ
12. Place		PONGO	PUSE
13. Know	SABER		SUPE
14. Have	TENER		TUVE

Bilingual Anagrams / Anagramas bilingües

Past Participles ★ Los participios

1.	SACKEBODUSE	SEEK	BUSCADO
2.	ROPINEABOTE	OPEN	ABIERTO
3.	GADIRTISOTA	STIR	AGITADO
4.	DANKOWALAD	WALK	ANDADO
5.	MOSKAFUMEDO	SMOKE	FUMADO
6.	SAROMYCADAR	MARRY	CASADO
7.	JOLAREWOBAD	LOWER	BAJADO
8.	TAGINOBRÍRD	BRING	TRAÍDO
9.	DOVALOMEA	LOVE	AMADO
10.	ZONEJADYOGO	ENJOY	GOZADO
11.	MACOTIDEO	EAT	COMIDO
12.	WECIRSITTERO	WRITE	ESCRITO
13.	CESAHIDUPEO	ESCAPE	HUIDO
14.	LÍFOALDAC	FALL	CAÍDO
15.	EDAVILESALO	LEAVE	SALIDO
16.	GUDALPOJAY	PLAY	JUGADO
17.	KINBEDRIDOB	DRINK	BEBIDO
18.	VASOWALHAD	WASH	LAVADO
19.	PADOYALHUDE	HELP	AYUDADO
20.	RUDYMABOPOC	BUY	COMPRADO

Labyrinth / Laberinto

Relative Pronouns and Other Words ★ Pronombres relativos y otras palabras

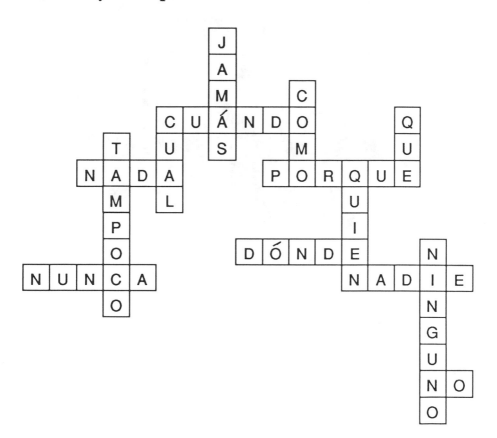

When?, CUÁNDO; Because, PORQUE; Where?, DÓNDE; Who, QUIEN; As, like, COMO; That, QUE; Which, CUAL; Never (#1), JAMÁS; Never (#2), NUNCA; Nobody, NADIE; Nothing, NADA; None, NINGUNO; Neither, TAMPOCO; No, NO.

Bilingual Crossword / Crucigrama bilingüe

Adjectives ★ Adjetivos

Drop and Add / Quite y añada

Infinitives ★ Infinitivos

1 English	2 Spanish	3 −	4 +	5 Spanish	6 English
1. To eat	COMER	C	T	METRO	Meter
2. To fall	CAER	R	J	CEJA	Eyebrow
3. To use	USAR	U	T	TRAS	After
4. To read	LEER	R	V	LEVE	Light
5. To bind	ATAR	T	S	ASAR	To roast
6. To dare	OSAR	R	E	ASEO	Cleanliness
7. To smell	OLER	L	C	CERO	Zero
8. To flee	HUIR	H	N	UNIR	To unite
9. To scratch	RAYAR	Y	J	RAJAR	To split
10. To erase	BORRAR	R	T	BROTAR	To sprout
11. To love	AMAR	M	P	PARA	For
12. To hear	OÍR	O	A	RÍA	Estuary

5

Word Cross / Palabras cruzadas
Families ★ Familias

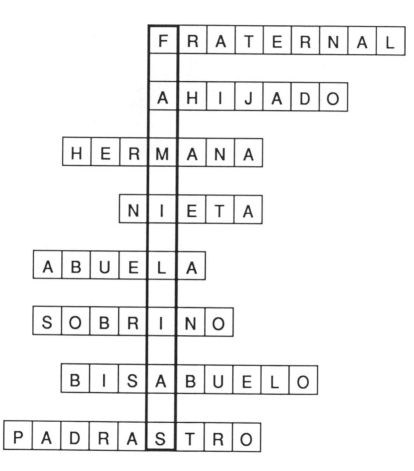

Granddaughter, NIETA; Sister, HERMANA; Nephew, SOBRINO; Brotherly, FRATERNAL; Stepfather, PADRASTRO; Great grandfather, BISABUELO; Godson, AHIJADO; Grandmother, ABUELA.

Labyrinth / Laberinto

The Family ★ La familia

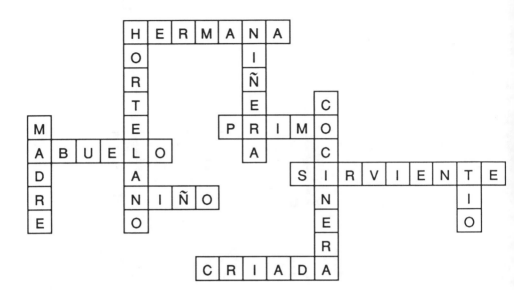

Sister, HERMANA; Child, NIÑO; Nursemaid, NIÑERA; Mother, MADRE; Gardener, HORTELANO; Maid, CRIADA; Cook, COCINERA; Uncle, TÍO; Servant, SIRVIENTE; Grandfather, ABUELO; Cousin, PRIMO.

World Search / Buscapalabras

At the Hospital ★ En el hospital

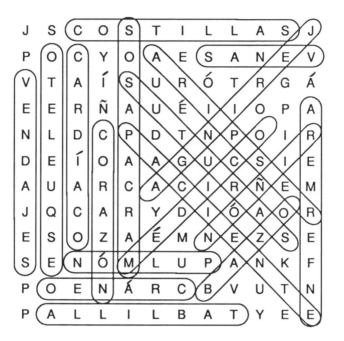

Bandages	VENDAJES	Lung	PULMÓN
Splint	TABLILLA	Heart	CORAZÓN
Patient	PACIENTE	Spleen	BAZO
Breathe	RESPIRA	Kidney	RIÑÓN
Syringe	JERINGA	Veins	VENAS
Doctor	MÉDICO	Skeleton	ESQUELETO
Pacemakers	MARCAPASOS	Ribs	COSTILLAS
Of the heart	CARDÍACO	Nurse	ENFERMERA
Sutures	SUTURAS	Skull	CRÁNEO

Bilingual Anagrams / Anagramas bilingües

Time and Weather ★ La hora y el tiempo

1.	GONETHINCH	NIGHT	NOCHE
2.	TILGYERCUNOS	CENTURY	SIGLO
3.	VIARUNILLA	RAIN	LLUVIA
4.	ADEFATECH	DATE	FECHA
5.	ILOCEHIE	ICE	HIELO
6.	JOLCELKORC	CLOCK	RELOJ
7.	DULBENUCO	CLOUD	NUBE
8.	ALIRADYIDIO	DAILY	DIARIO
9.	FACHORCARSTES	FROST	ESCARCHA
10.	MEPOTIMEIT	TIME	TIEMPO
11.	GIEFOBALN	FOG	NIEBLA
12.	WORÍCEDO	DEW	ROCÍO
13.	NSHEMOTM	MONTH	MES
14.	DEWIVONTIN	WIND	VIENTO
15.	LORCÍFOD	COLD	FRÍO
16.	WENOVISEN	SNOW	NIEVE
17.	RAYOÑEA	YEAR	AÑO
18.	HARBEDSAMOS	SHADE	SOMBRA
19.	DRONTEHURNUTE	THUNDER	TRUENO
20.	KAMEWENASE	WEEK	SEMANA

Labyrinth / Laberinto

At the Table ★ En la mesa

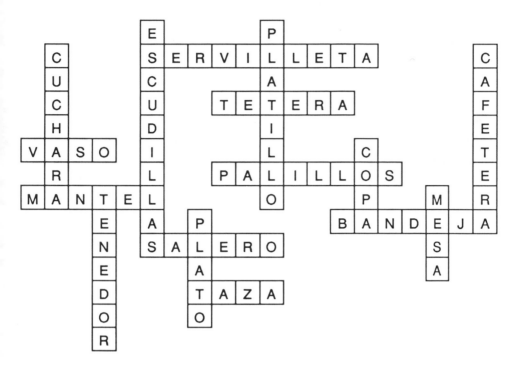

Napkin, SERVILLETA; Saucer, PLATILLO; Bowls, ESCUDILLAS; Spoon, CUCHARA; Goblet, COPA; Tablecloth, MANTEL; Toothpicks, PALILLOS; Glass, VASO; Saltshaker, SALERO; Teapot, TETERA; Table, MESA; Plate, PLATO; Tray, BANDEJA; Fork, TENEDOR; Cup, TAZA; Coffeepot, CAFETERA.

Drop and Add / Quite y añada

The Home ★ La casa

1 English	2 Spanish	3 −	4 +	5 Spanish	6 English
1. Mirror	ESPEJO	J	S	ESPESO	Thick
2. Bed	CAMA	M	V	VACA	Cow
3. Table	MESA	E	A	MASA	Dough
4. Bath	BAÑO	B	D	DAÑO	Harm
5. Tub	TINA	I	A	NATA	Cream
6. House	CASA	C	L	SALA	Living room
7. Floor	PISO	I	E	PESO	Mexican money
8. Clock	RELOJ	L	Z	ROJEZ	Redness
9. Chair	SILLA	S	V	VILLA	Small town
10. AM/FM	RADIO	I	B	BARDO	Bard
11. Courtyard	PATIO	I	S	PASTO	Grass
12. Balcony	BALCÓN	B	H	HALCÓN	Falcon

6

Word Cross / Palabras cruzadas

Recreation ★ El recreo

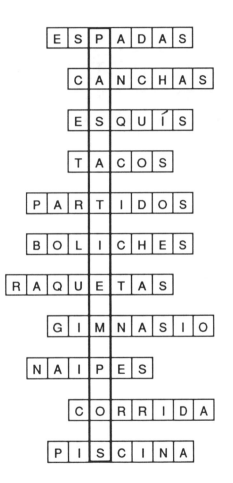

Swords (fencing), ESPADAS; Games (soccer), PARTIDOS; Playing cards, NAIPES; Tennis equipment, RAQUETAS; Billiard cues, TACOS; Gym, GIMNASIO; Bullfight, CORRIDA; Tennis courts, CANCHAS; Bowling balls, BOLICHES; Skis, ESQUÍS; Swimming pool, PISCINA.

Word Search / Buscapalabras

Buildings and Arenas ★ Edificios y ruedos

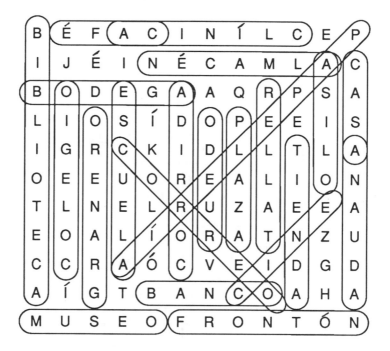

Post office	**CORREO**	
Medical building	**CLÍNICA**	
Wine cellar/shop	**BODEGA**	
Library	**BIBLIOTECA**	
Arena	**RUEDO**	
Barn	**GRANERO**	
Movie theater	**CINE**	
School	**ESCUELA**	
Store	**TIENDA**	
Bullfight	**CORRIDA**	
Bank	**BANCO**	

Museum	**MUSEO**
Academy	**COLEGIO**
Town square	**PLAZA**
Coffee shop	**CAFÉ**
Customs	**ADUANA**
Warehouse	**ALMACÉN**
Asylum	**ASILO**
House	**CASA**
Jai alai court	**FRONTÓN**
Stationery shop	**PAPELERÍA**
Workshop	**TALLER**

Bilingual Anagrams / Anagramas bilingües

Amusement ★ Diversiones

1.	RAFITYSEPAT	PARTY	FIESTA
2.	SHERZEAJSEDC	CHESS	AJEDREZ
3.	IROCELUISEO	LEISURE	OCIO
4.	LAVEJIRAVATR	(To) TRAVEL	VIAJAR
5.	MAJOSEGUSEG	GAMES	JUEGOS
6.	SACHIGEPSNIF	FISHING	PESCA
7.	DAWIRAMNS	(To) SWIM	NADAR
8.	KUISEQÍS	SKI	ESQUÍ
9.	LABECINADE	DANCE	BAILE
10.	EVONCIMIE	MOVIE	CINE
11.	CROSCIRCUCI	CIRCUS	CIRCO
12.	GUNZATHINAC	HUNTING	CAZA
13.	BÓFINCHIBOYA	HOBBY	AFICIÓN
14.	RAFAIRFIE	FAIR	FERIA
15.	NATEKSAPIRAT	(To) SKATE	PATINAR
16.	JILBOKSACECH	JACKS	BOLICHE
17.	PANSERCAIDS	CARDS	NAIPES
18.	TÓLBALNOFOLAB	FOOTBALL	BALÓN
19.	SERDOPTOPERT	SPORT	DEPORTE
20.	EFARDELISDAPE	PARADE	DESFILE

Bilingual Crossword / Crucigrama bilingüe

Leisure Time ★ Tiempo libre

Drop and Add / Quite y añada

Having Fun ★ Divirtiéndose

1 English	2 Spanish	3 −	4 +	5 Spanish	6 English
1. Leisure	OCIO	C	G	OIGO	I hear
2. Bat (baseball)	BATE	B	M	TEMA	Theme
3. Art	ARTE	E	A	RATA	Rat
4. Hunting	CAZA	Z	R	CARA	Face
5. Movie theater	CINE	C	B	BIEN	Well
6. Court (tennis)	CANCHA	A	O	CONCHA	Shell
7. To read	LEER	R	V	LEVE	Light (weight)
8. Track	PISTA	S	R	PITAR	To whistle
9. Dance	BAILE	E	R	ABRIL	April
10. Circus	CIRCO	R	N	CINCO	Five
11. To swim	NADAR	R	Z	DANZA	Dancing
12. Boat	BARCO	R	N	BANCO	Bank